ROADS TO NOWHERE

Poems and short stories

by

Les Padfield

Printed in Victoria, BC, Canada

Note for Librarians: a cataloguing record for this book that includes Dewey Decimal Classification and US Library of Congress numbers is available from the Library and Archives of Canada. The complete cataloguing record can be obtained from their online database at:
www.collectionscanada.ca/amicus/index-e.html
ISBN 1-4120-2972-4

TRAFFORD

This book was published *on-demand* in cooperation with Trafford Publishing. On-demand publishing is a unique process and service of making a book available for retail sale to the public taking advantage of on-demand manufacturing and Internet marketing. On-demand publishing includes promotions, retail sales, manufacturing, order fulfilment, accounting and collecting royalties on behalf of the author.

Offices in Canada, USA, UK, Ireland, and Spain
book sales for North America and international:
Trafford Publishing, 6E–2333 Government St.
Victoria, BC V8T 4P4 CANADA
phone 250 383 6864   toll-free 1 888 232 4444
fax 250 383 6804   email to orders@trafford.com
book sales in Europe:
Trafford Publishing (UK) Ltd., Enterprise House, Wistaston Road Business Centre
Crewe, Cheshire CW2 7RP UNITED KINGDOM
phone 01270 251 396   local rate 0845 230 9601
facsimile 01270 254 983   orders.uk@trafford.com
order online at:
www.trafford.com/robots/04-0800.html

10   9   8   7   6   5   4   3   2

Dedicated to s a n a

and the Inca Trekkers

Roads to nowhere,
Leading nowhere,
Making tracks
for someone else to tread...

(song lyric)

All profits from this book will be donated to two charities: Action Aid and The Coombe Trust.

Thanks are due to Anthony Conway and Tim Barnes for the layout and completion of this book.

Contents

POEMS

Contents

Contents

SHORT STORIES

The Parable of the Talents

In adolescence
arsenal ignored him,
ringo beat him to the bongos,
haemorrhoids destroyed
his chances of olympic fame...

In maturity
rada remained unimpressed
at his stunning macbeth,
the tate declared his nouveau
futurism just too late,
and even cliff refused
to sing his composition blues...

Now moribund
he writes us rhyme,
convinced by time we
wouldn't recognise
real genius
even if it screamed at us.

Programmed

For Thine
is the kingdom,
The power and the glory,
For ever and ever. Amen.

Enter.

Intensive Care

Three years past.

Passed in bits of broken time,
Day on thin day falling at a window.
And all questions have been asked,
The monosyllables of each old line
   recording that your shadow stopped
   and touched me for a time.

And now has passed.

Like litter in a street love drops
Defaced, disfiguring;
Each neat apology encased
In litany, disguising your discarding
   of a token hope
   once taken, once refused.

Old, broken, used.

As suns and summers rise
And fingers fan to find
No hand, no meeting mind,
Time lies and laughs and scans
   your acid promise
   of a vile eternity.

And sadness reaches up like bile.

Rape in progress
(Cheviot View)

For a thousand years
or more
the leaves of trees brushed moody skies.

And for a thousand years
more
the hill, grassed with green,
knew
the innocent touch
of grey or blue.

Now, between the breaking
and the waking of wild flowers,
in a thousand hours
or less
the penetrating steel subdues,
denudes,
gouges out the brown bowels,
lays them in lumps
besides the calculated lines
designed to speed away
the excrement from tinted azure suites.

And in a thousand hours more
will pour the aerialed cars,
the jewellery, the cigars,
the desperate little batch appreciative
of meretricious nuance;
voyeurs panting for Exclusive

plots to hatch,
numbed by desire against
plain
exquisite silence
lying underneath.

No Option

so
what's left
on a wet monday
bank holiday afternoon
when you've done the museums
visited all the world's garden centres
read every gripping novel in the house
been bored by the snooker and old films on the tele
and made phone calls to friends who aren't there but sex ?

Weak End

If

Sunday night

was

Saturday night

then

everything would be

alright

on Monday.

Returning Summer

One by one they will return
Throttling down across forgotten fields
To taxi up beside abandoned huts.

And down the lanes, now bramble-choked,
The women and the men, on foot, on bike,
Drift lazily as summer breezes, voices light.

Tired limbs seek out the sanctuary of earth
As from the cockpit they emerge, greeting
Dust like Lazarus, at least for one more day.

Some stumble, others flex
And look around to meet and mingle,
Keeping at arms length the absentees.

The morning rays spear down and cling
Half-shimmering, on the blue-grey cloth.
The smoke of cigarettes ascends, defiant

From the lanes, now redolent with heat,
As men and women push through broken gates
To trace their steps across the pitted ground,

Along the tarmac, unsubdued by earth,
To join the silent shuffling figures stinking sweat
And rubber, kerosene and cheated death.

One by one they may return
To meet again the waiting aching hearts,
Drink deeply from the wells of loss.

Or from the open sky, like silent birds,
The beautiful and burnt may soar together,
Moulded by a haze of time and terror,

Wearing guilt like medals. Culpable.
Inviolable. Uncertain for all time
If they should land again today, next year, or never.

Bobby Moore

1942-93
Captain of England

When in those years to come
Our children and their children
Wonder why we speak of him
In hallowed tones,
What shall we say
Of what we now must know?

That he was one who shunned
The brashy trickery of flick and flash,
Whose turn of speed would not amaze,
Who did not dazzle with exploding fire -
And yet whose mark was unsurpassed,
Whose better we have yet to see.
A gentle, iron soul with skill of steel,
With matching grace and monumental calm.
A master and a man with more to teach
Than we, in all our seeking, dared absorb.
Who reached and held the stars of fame,
Replacing each unsullied and unstained.

And in those far-off heady summer days
He carried for us
More than all we wanted then:
In lifting gold he lifted us,
Not as our transient superstar
But captain of us all.

We may not dare pretend
We knew him through and through.
But in the going of this friend
A part of all of us goes too.
And when in future times they ask us why,
Let special silent memories give reply.

The Church Hall

Yawning empty, here it stays
smelling of sawdust, cloth and polish.
Sands of time scrubbed clean around
Peeling, flaking, whitewashed walls.

What lines of local fame,
Parochial embarrassments,
Have stepped across this unfit stage,
Extracting pleasure
From adoring undiscerners,
Drunk with filial pride.

Brown-keyed piano
Coloured by neglect,
Stained ivory like a smoker's teeth
Leans, terminally tuneless,
Not To Be Opened,
Awaiting its final movement.

Space of pageants and parades,
Saluting worlds of uniforms
And dances, shuttlecocks,
Most useful knots, of
Sales and fayres and minor meetings
Grey-hat widows serving squash and
Tea from urns and fairy cakes.
Pinned information, faded, torn,
On Semaphore and Morse,
An old and dated double act.

Free now of sounds and scrapes.
Unthreatened by intemperate youths
High-kicking balls to crashing lights.

All final unsold rags long cleared
From wooden trestle tables, stacked high.
No Next Time, even for the paperback Cheyneys.

Last game of the long day. Ripped curtains closed.
Flags lowered. Music silenced.

Waiting for the epilogue.

First November

The ragged limping night came creeping down
The silent lakeland lanes with measured tread.
The shadow of his drifting raven gown
Reflecting in the charcoal sky he fed.
We wandered back enshrouded by the road,
Eyes laughing, glancing from the far unturned,
Complete and unafraid as though we strode
In unseen unison, the night adjourned.
Like random children who have scaled the heights
We held together in unchartered lands,
Closed eyes and minds to warning winter nights
And wrapped our futures in a clasp of hands.
So cast the dye beyond recovery;
First touch of love. Love's first discovery.

Ill Wind

Seven on a

Spring evening.

Sitting in a

Scottish garden

Sipping

Sunshine sparkled wine.

Global warming?
Two lumps please.

Garth

Old man Garth,
Sitting, smoking alone,
Aged and wrinkled – waiting to die.
Stumbling and coughing and yawning and sleeping.
Rich enough to live in comfort :
What use your money now, old man ?
No-one to care
Or understand that muddled mind.
A pack of cards his sole companion
As Patience plays away his life.

Saturday will bring his son
For one brief hour. Moments
Spent in tedious duty, minus even a façade
Of interest or concern. Moments spent
To make sure that old Garth
Won't leave his money to the Sailors' Home.

The mournful bloodhound look
That hints he wants to say so much
Is turned back to his old gold watch
To see his life tick slowly by.

What thoughts meander through that hazy brain ?
What memories or hopes persist ?
A fear of death ? A fear of life ?
No hope of Heaven
No dread of Hell.

Sleep on in fitful starts, old man
Until the night when sleep will claim you.
Nature's miracle forced to follow Nature's way.
Sleep on for just a little while.

Black and White

The reel spluttered,
  hiccoughed
  into a freezing
  failure.
Pandemonium erupted like part of the script.

Boos and howls,
  unwanted light; barked warnings
  from the capped commissionaire
  who in his youth
  dodged bullets on a Dunkirk beach,
  now to be pinged in the neck
  by a guided peanut.
  Exit the nearest door
  with eyes watering from a twisted ear:
  The Wrong Suspect.

Bored munching in the unplanned gap.
We ducked from harm's way as sweets
And chewed gum flayed randomly, wondering
If this was a money-back day.

And then: Re-birth.
  Cheering babble drowning conversation
  from the crowd
  in the corner of the smoky saloon
  where the shark palms the ace
  and the table is upturned before
Pandemonium erupts as part of the script.

A bottle breaks across a head,
the wooden banister gives way
beneath embattled bodies and bashes out a tune
onto the honky-tonk beneath.
Madam in her swishing dress emerges from an upstairs
room
in time to see a body slide torpedo-like along the bar,
and some bit-part unknown is thrown out
through the swinging doors into the dusty street
never to be seen again until next fall.

It's a good fight; no-one
needing stitches or counselling.

We knew the Indian attacks, though wild,
Would be repelled, with Sioux and Cheyenne falling
bloodless from their horses as the Cavalry emerged,
spick uniforms and spicker timing,
to save and civilise...

Tom Mix, Roy Rogers or The Cisco Kid.
No disputing who to love or who would lose -
The bully, mean and shifty eyed,
 moustached and always clad in black,
 told once and only once by Hopalong –
 (just arrived and passing through) –
 to Get Out Of Town !
 (even though he'd lived there all his life).

It's a good line: no-one arguing,
or taking up the case for Compensation.

And after clear cathartic cuffing
We poured out into the coloured sunlit
Weekend world and galloped home
Down dusty streets,
Untroubled by equivocation,
Bullet blazing fingers,
Killing off the chasing pack
Whose arrows caused us no concern,
Knowing we were on the side of Right.

13.3.96

The searing sound of pain:
A mother wailing
for her murdered child.

Double it. And
double it again
and double it
and double it
again, again....

Dunblane.

Forgotten in an old and hidden book

Forgotten
in an old and hidden book
I found two letters,
creased with secrecy,
undusted by discovery.

I read of long and longing love,
whispering across the years;
of parting tears and seas
of separation
breached by moments of
mad hope and pulsing expectation.

*   *   *   *

I glimpse him, writer and recipient,
sitting sinking in his thoughts.
I catch his glaze and wonder
on what tumbled ecstasy it stalks,
what soundless hurt lies hidden
tumourous inside his soul.

I fold his letter : he folds his life.
And both lie creased and dusty,
stuffed between the pages
of a fiction many know,
as if by heart they learn.

Night Fears

Night falls.
Fears rise.
And all that reassures
Evaporates into the inky skies.
The solid certainties of light
Now crack and start to splinter in defeat
Against the creeping black.
Bravado, like a toothless mutt,
Lies cowed and whimpering
Inside the gut
Whilst Action bows submissively
To Impotence, and gropes its way
To know if day will ever follow night
Or night quench day

Farvey

His half-smiling sepia face
peers out at me
across the space that
passes for his daughter's room.

Farvey.

   Solid, now silent, grey figure
in a dark passage way.
Coming in from a smoggy winter night,
dressed in a trilby,
taking and making my mouth organ sing.
Sitting me on his lap
beside a Christmas tree,
pregnant with presents and lighted pine.
Talking with others of Past, and Peace
that I, God-willing, should inherit.

Farvey.

   I cannot hear your voice, cannot
feel the love you held for me, nor
remember more the years that
you were there
before I saw, from across
the street, the white sheet at the window;
entered the hushed house
to be imprisoned in whispered, anguished,

incoherent tales
of angels, as though I had
not yet heard of
Death, or knew its grip...

She passes me a book,
Gold-letters dull on faded red.
- No interest to anybody now -
  no one will want it
   so I'll put it out.

A thousand names -
A sample's sample of those who lived and died -
And you were there:
Rank. History. Address.
My grey, mouth organ playing
trilby-hatted Farvey.

Playing out your youth at Ypres,
Somme and Passchendale.
Arras, Albert, Neuve Chappelle.
Not one, but all the names
of history - your history .
My history!
With medals, long since lost, she says,
tokens which you never wore:
swore that you would never put them on
because – though scarred and gassed and hurt -
you came back.
Keeping secret all
the whys and wheres.

But I know, Farvey.
Because I too was there,
surviving with you. Your life. My life.
Two ends of a stick,
not one without the other.
Joined by the common sap
that ran between us when you sat me on your lap
and told me tales of Peace.

The Other Cheek
(K.A.Crawford FRDS)

That's the trouble with people like you !

If someone Outside -
   in the street
   on a bus or at a party
   caused me this sort of aggro
   and pain
   and discomfort
   they'd get a punch;
   or a push;
   or at least a good blast of insult.

In Here
   there's no retaliation
   no fighting back no answering back
   just lying there seething inside
   looking up at the light
   or the mr men mobiles or the hairs up your nose
   while you take liberties
   cracking jokes with your half-competent assistant:
   "now for the other side...."

And then
   I smile and thank you.
   Smile ! And *thank you* !
   and book again
   for my annual check
   and your annual cheque.

I was OK before I came in here.
  No aches and pains.
  No numb nose. And I could talk.

But I'll get even.
  You wait till I see my friends.
  You wait till I tell them about you !

Analogy

Unrequited love
is like TB :
It leaves you holes
where living used to be.

Love on Toast

In the deep
releasing
shadow-ridden night,
when noise is banished
and light is slowed
to mellow-toning sleep,
I write you words
of tender and unceasing love....

They reach you
in the morning post
when lines are semi-noted
between frenzied
gulps
of coffee,
bites of toast
and folded to be
glimpsed again
between the Mail
and Cosmopolitan
on the busy bumpy 8.03

Ball by Ball

If gully's diving catch
should save the match
and square the series;
Or if the opening bowler wearies
in the morning heat and sees
the bouncer hooked with ease

Be sure the pictured words will catch it:

ball
  by ball
      by
  ball
        by
ball.

With all the detail of a summer scene:
red on willow, white on green,
panoramic prose embracing
overthrows, frenetic chasing,
classic cutting, tail-end thumping,
run-outs, leg-befores and stumpings,

ball
  by ball
      by
  ball
        by
ball

The fall of every wicket raising
voices, scornful, praising;
anecdotes of spin and pace,
of records batting back to Grace;
of rowdy crowds and comments yelled
at streaking extroverts expertly felled

ball
  by ball
      by
ball
        by
ball.

Be sure the pictured words will catch it:

Catch and capture frames
of ungrown boys in timeless games;
tension-lazy, mirth-inspired
halcyon heroics wired
over distant boundaries, minding play
till one more summer slips away,

ball
 by
final ball.

Visitors to the Sculpture Show

Look at me, I stand much longer
Than the rest before each piece.
So expertly appreciative
In clothes that show my unique mix
Of anarchy and elegance.

You see, I understand the wit
In fishnets full of broken bulbs
The porno-painted potting shed
And that exquisite plastic nose job
Added to a Ghirlanlandaio.

I see just what it is that makes
This slightly melted monkey wrench
A poignant existentialist
Motif, the harsh emotive tension
That the bidet, squat and buddha-like
Can force on space.

Just look at me, you see
I never need a catalogue
Art has no mystery for me
Unlike for you barbarian posers
Only coming in because it's free.

Madverbs

insanely
naively

longingly
overwhelmingly
violently
eternally

wildly
impetuously
thrillingly
helplessly

yearningly
o but so so
unwisely!

One percent

For months, nothing.
  the well run dry,
  the last bus garaged.
  the phones silent.

Then from all directions
  Barrage. Unblocking.
  No turning a deserted corner,
  No opening a fridge door
  Without a metaphor met,
  Some simile similarly
  Flaunting itself, false-smiling,
  Like a red-lipped whore
  Demanding payment,
  Scratching at the dog-tired hours
  Pledged elsewhere,
  Before smirking away,
  Free of all responsibility,
  Leaving behind
  Much unsatisfied
  Unfinished business.

Delivered

Other people's smiles she mirrors,
echoes their broad warmth
and gushing glowing admiration
for new and pulsing blood.

Now she will be spurred to make
the christening shawl, the cake;
she will assume her honorary place
with pose and picture-smiling face.

But as she takes off
shoes and laddered stockings,
sits singly on the edge
of her only ever bed,
she shuts her eyes
for tearing pain she's never known,
the weight she's never borne:
for skin and smell to stain
the soleness that torments
and tourniquets her life.
And when the darkness meets her
it is not infant cries
but maiden tears that
steal the sleeping hours
and mock her barren years.

An Inspector Calls

And in came the inspector
with rose-tinted bi-focals
half-way down her nose, platinum
blond hair and tweed bum....

with clipboard and setinstone smile
she sat at the back of the room
next to the rat Mackessy whose messy book
she looked through noticing it
hadn't been marked for a month but
not knowing the little tyke rarely wandered in...

sat there observing, scribbling
away under lurid dyed eyebrows
until the bell went and she
debriefed me...

must never kill creative urges insisting on such dated dull
irrelevancies
as paragraphs and punctuation why are you not trying out
the method
teaching from the back whilst standing on your head surely
you know that
studies from the university of the isle of frogs has proved it
thirteen point
four more effective than traditional methods...

I nod mutely, unprotesting,
for I want to be seen to be Progressive,
and climb with her upstairs, glimpsing
her startled rapture at the noise of blind stampeding
boots that bowl her down a flight,
and at the bottom catch the first smear
trickling into the setinblood smile
as she comes to a full stop standing on her head.

Other Lines

The drone of conversation mingles
monotone monoxide traffic:
heavy air and heavy lids.

And through an open window
a mile away
beyond the reddened roofs,
the silent snaking of a train,
slow-moving train
heading empty
coastwards,
not fridaynight-full,
bank-holiday bursting,
but sweet forbidden
emptiness,
delicious truant
loneliness.

The drone of conversation mingles
monotone monoxide traffic:
heavy air and heavy life.

Gerald

To those of us left watching in the crowd
It seems unfair that you were given Out.
But as you would have probably avowed
We beat the air
Unknowing, unaware.
This Umpire always has the final shout.

Conversely Speaking

There's nothing worse that I can think of -
    (large bum on bus seat,
    flabby fingers reach
    to steady bulging bag as
    gears grind away,
    drizzle drips along steamed window,
    traffic treacles in the evening crawl) -
than supermarket shopping on a Friday night.
Nightmare. Hate it. Can't abide it.
Specially when the trolley won't push right !

The rains failed and the well dried up.
We walked an hour on burning soil with
Plastic buckets. And then an hour back.
And for the day and for the year
Eked out our chances, never knowing
When the drops would come. And in
The evening shadows we would sit
And would have thirstily complained
Of trolleys hard to push and crowds
That made it tedious to queue,
If only we had known.

The Ward

The dimmed insomniac light
curls itself around grunts and snores
and farts and moans as
night is measured by each aching throb
in head and bowel.

Across the floor a jaundiced Jew
with face and eyes like ripe lemon peel
spills Yiddish dreams into the pressing night;
night gulped in with relish
by the ebullient banker coming
to the end of his historic hernia;
and coming to the end, deflated in his skin,
with tubes draining and claiming the life juice,
a sack of a man, moustached, masticated,
like an old white Gandhi.

Here the comic meets the legless,
the well-travelled publisher displays himself,
the token Pole keeps his face and history blanketed,
the General craves for lost salutes.

Here Respect is what is hidden under sheets,
is carried only by the clean young girls and men
who joke beneath their glasses and their masks;
by those whose turn it is not yet to be
sliced and cut on slabs, stuffed like
festive hens until the living and the artificial merge.

Old men suspend millennium's pride
with untutored exhibitions of pads
and pans and penises while no-one says
they mind if you piss in the bath or on the floor,
for here everyone knows what you are
and what you can become.

Arranged Marriage

The bouquets are arranged.

And because the bouquets are arranged
we will perform
the binding blinding ritual,
dismember and unite in white
forgetting it is life
we push away,
for mounds of time to cover thoughts
of parted lips and fingertips,
of loving hands on living hills
clasping passing secrets.

We will not shock or disappoint
the crowds who wait with stones.
We will begin
the bending blending ritual
and smother each defiant spark
that threatens us with light.

The long belonging ritual will run.
But as you pass across the street
I will not greet your glance
for fear I understand it.

Angel Guardians

Where were her angels
on that night
when manic menace
took away her Beauty
Youth
Life ?

Where but where
were those
angels sent to guard her
from the savage
ravaged wreck
that ripped away her
Youth
Life ?

Were there angels sleeping
angels weeping
on that night that sanctioned
stark and forcing dark
to devastate all Life ?

Witnesses: Simon of Cyrene

I know why they choose me.
Not because I'm big and strong.
They see the blackness of my face, my arms and body.
Black, they think, we'll use the Black.

I ask them what is going on:
This is not my city,
not my country,
these Jews and Romans, not my people.
But still they drag me into
their affairs,
their politics and vengeances.

The man already is half dead.
I see the whip marks on his back,
the bruises on his face where
beatings have been given,
his hair blood-matted from the thorns
pushed hard into his skull.
There's little mercy
on the road to execution.

Instinctively I baulk, refuse, protest.
Why should I carry such a thing,
a mark of shame, disgust,
for some abandoned criminal ?
But guards are rarely prone to argue.

It is heavy enough,
heavy even for a man my size,
and as I wrest it from beneath,

he stumbles to his knees.
A soldier kicks him to his feet :
I hear some laughter from the watching crowd.
And I feel sick.

At the rubbish dump
I'm told to drop the cross
so they can finish off the business.
For the first time then,
I meet his eyes.

'Thank you,' he says.

He thanks me for carrying his cross.
I barely believe it,
but it is in his eyes
as well as on his lips.

I cannot stay to watch the horror.
Away I hear the hammers
and the cries of pain.
Inside I should be feeling shame
at what I have been forced to do.
And yet it is not like that.
I do not feel abused or sullied
like you might suppose.
But do not ask me to explain.
It is not something that I understand...

Witnesses: Pilate

You can think what you like,
but you don't have to make the decisions.
Do you.
In an ideal world I would have just
released the man,
of course I would.
Anyone could see it was a set up,
a put up job by those infernal priests,
and all,
as far as I could see,
about some petty Jewish squabbles
all about their damn religion.
Why they take such things so seriously
I'll never understand.

I really did feel sorry for the man.
I don't know what he'd done -
I guess he'd smashed a couple of their rituals,
called himself their king or something.
Nothing in my book to warrant death
and that's for sure.
But then he didn't really help himself,
remaining silent to my questions.
I mean, it was as though he didn't realise
the authority I had,
the power of life and death
that I held over him.
Perhaps I had not realised
the depth of hatred piled against him.
I thought they might be satisfied
with just a flogging.

I even had the brilliant gem
of resurrecting an obscure concession
we once used,
releasing some convicted Jew
to please them at their Feast time.

But no, no, no.
They wanted blood,
his blood,
and that's for sure.
Nothing short of death would do.

You have to weigh things quickly at a time like this.
The crowd could easily turn nasty, and what then ?
Send in the troops ?
So dozens, maybe hundreds die,
And many just as innocent as this one man.
No one in their right mind would make that choice.

He's not the first to suffer death
expediently upon some gallows.
And he won't be the last.
A few days more and it will all die down.
Next week you won't be able to recall his name.
It's politics.
A dirty business, politics.

You just don't understand...

Witnesses: A woman

I should be weeping, but I'm numb.

For over five hours now
I've stood here with Salome, Mary,
other women,
holding one another fast
for comfort,
unable to look up and see the suffering ;
unable just to look away.
I don't know what to do or what to feel.

The men have gone,
except his closest friends.
Some women in the crowd abuse us;
most ignore our vigil.
The faces of a few show pity, sometimes guilt.
They know as well as we do
that it's wrong.

It makes no sense.

To kill or rob brings punishment.
He taught us love, forgiveness.

Forgiveness which encompassed me!
Changed and gave me hope for better things.

For that, they hang him on a tree,
let killers mingle with the crowd,
as free as air.

It makes no sense

We'll stand here till it's over.
God willing it can't last much longer.
Rumours in the crowd are mouthed
about this sudden darkness spelling doom,
and stories from the city of strange things
within the temple walls....

For us, though, standing here,
these things wash over.
We grieve our separate ways,
but not one of us understands...

Rhyme

What rhymes with a Broken Heart :

a knife in the side

the weight that bends

the poison in the blood

the hole in the chest

the suffocating mist

the stopping of time

the vacant tomorrow

the bland and banal

the darkness of dawn

a knife inside

that finally

Finally

Rips

Apart.

Base Line

If
    after much discussion
    on the virtues of democracy
    of disenfranchised rights contesting
    with Establishment's hypocrisy
    in constantly reverting
    to authoritarian values and regimes
    to bolster flawed perverting
    ideologies and thereby keep the
    status quo
you still won't go to bed
I'll give you such a wallop
that you'll travel through that door
without your feet in contact with the floor.

Exchange Rate

Like a ring of bullies
the mountains crowd above
the dusty town, small and down.
Aguas Calientes.
Precocious in its boast:
trying to sound more
than just a progeny of discovery,
feeding off the scraps
that drift down from the temples
high above.

Devoid of beauty
it dresses to appeal,
moves easily to accommodate
the moneyed strangers
wondering in their wanderings.
The market, mute and patient,
squats awkwardly in the heat,
too proud to tout for trade;
or perhaps too lazy.

Its arteries and veins,
the river and the railway,
fetch and carry,
fetch and carry.
Young men, defiantly colourful,
with eyes and faces old as history
wait vacantly beside the rails
for their return
to the dawn's new burdens,
whilst bony dogs scrounge scraps

from sated visitors,
revelling in the strangeness of it all.
It is, after all,
a place of need,
which is why I am here.
Partly why I am here.
There is no mystery in poverty,
no glamour in the sandal taped together,
or the mud that covers minds and lives.

        *   *   *

Yet in the early evening schoolyard
I watch children moving
to the beat of an ancient rhythm.
A youth who whistles bangs a drum,
Berates a boy for awkwardness.
Mothers and others sit around
To watch with mild insouciance
The group devoid of inhibition,
Urgent in their simplicity.

Along the track the train halts
As if by arrangement.
I pull down a window
And throw sweets
To the fast-gathering children
Whose gabbling zest and appetite
Disturb and disconnect me.
There is no patronage
In my intention.
Only in my actions.
And reflected in the moving glass

That separates our worlds
The offerings seem suddenly obscene,
Like drops of poison poured into a well,
Waiting for the drawing day
When sweet taste is destruction.

Without conviction
The narrow train and I lurch on,
As if embarrassed to arrive too soon.
Much, much too soon.
We merge and then emerge
As harbingers of More,
With gift-wrapped drainage
For the clearing town,
Systems to enhance the ancient beat
And laws that will defeat
The frightening freedom of the careless child
Who ambles over an unguarded track
And goes back home alone.

As valleys suck away
The old god's dying light
The night swarms in,
Competing with the Urubamba
For the seat of ancient fear,
And I am questioned as a stranger who returns
If it is the snake or condor spirit I assist.
Coming to this place of need.
From this world of need.
And like the draining light
All sureness narrows to a speck,
Uncertain if what long ago
Began with greed
I will complete with charity.

Saturday Sport

Morning: Anticipation

Afternoon: Perspiration

Evening: Recrimination

Words on Play

Susie was a girl that I never made love to;
Sarah was a girl that I did.
Sally was defensive and eventually expensive;
Samantha did it all for just a quid.

Angela had qualms about giving up her charms;
Alice couldn't wait to kiss and tell.
Annie was so stunning that she took my breath away;
Amy took my credit cards as well.

Dawn began to yawn at the thought of going further,
Debbie dug her nails in deep.
Denise was into dating long before she started mating,
Diane simply went to bed to sleep.

All the blondes and the brunettes who made pleasure taste
sweet
And were captivated by my spell
Linger only in a mist, now untouched, unkissed.
I'm left here as lonely as hell.

Water Palace

glubbing garbled market of wet noise screaming girls
and bare-backed boys yellow-shirted gargoyle guard
self-important fit and hard aqua zooms and rubber rings
beating music wave machines flabby mothers bosomed
gran macho muscled hairy man ostentatious dive proof
tan all enclosed protected guarded garbled fun in
sunless coldless windless rainless siren screaming
chlorinated globule swamp of human flab...

gurgle hubble squabble trouble
round about the cauldron bubble
hell in liquid form.

Supergeddon

One day soon the world will end.

Not in the reigning down of bombs
But at a supermarket checkout
where
a bar code
can't
be found.
And all
the universe
will
congregate
and linger
there
in
one
eternal
mumbling
grumbling
stretching
to infinitylong queueueueueueueueu.....

Doc's Diary

Doc Hall
who taught us French
would pace and pace
between the space
of wooden desk and bench
instructing us in Gaelic Gaul
to conjugate, digest, recall.

And in
a moment's pause
he'd often scan
his private diary, plan
events, the weekly cause,
the concert trip, the Sunday spin,
the school exchange to Saint-Thurin.

One day
he failed to show.
A sudden stroke
took him before he woke.
Good way to end it; though
I bet his diary didn't say
he planned to spend the day away.

Not Stopping at St. John's

Leaving behind
my gliding chair,
moulded, black-tubular
I quit
My brightly lit
Carpet-plushed
Japonica scented nine-to-five
And glide down
In the gliding lift with tuneful sound
To trace a mere few hundred
Paces to the charing centre
Of the hubbub universal cross in
Just sufficient time to take
A place among the faces
Liberty Bound.

Platform four
The eighteen ten
First class
To Waterloo and London Bridge
Then fast to Tunbridge Wells,
All's well it's fast to
Tunbridge fast to Tunbridge Wells,
Not touching earth till Tunbridge Wells,
Not refuelling, not reloading or replenishing
And not stopping at St. John's.

Between the earth and Tunbridge Wells
No views,
No distant worthwhile hues
To warrant raised or open eyes.

No expectation or distraction
Needing to be viewed
Beyond reflection.
Just a journey across space
A void
Another place
Devoid of comprehension.

*   *   *

A traveller once related tales
Of people living far but near,
Whose hopes and journeys mirrored mine,
With trains that ran on shorter lines,
But never reached the leafy glades
Or pleasant shades of twisted vines
And far horizons,
Way beyond the confines of St.John's.

Too frightening and too fanciful
To think it could be true.

*   *   *

All's well it's fast to
Tunbridge fast to Tunbridge Wells,
Not seeing earth till Tunbridge Wells,
Not leaving, not believing,
And not stopping at St.John's.

Road to Somewhere

For twenty weeks
You feel it with increasing ache;

For thirty hours bear the pain
Of tearing flesh;

For forty years
Lose sleep and hair and memory;

All this for some small helpless scrap
Of noisy wet humanity

To which you whisper, warn and promise:
 I will never cease to love you

Lacking
                    logic
             common-sense
                  intelligence
          financial acumen
                 health and
            peace of mind and
                    sleep
               and more,

But leading Somewhere, that's for sure.

SHORT
STORIES

PICTURE PICTURE

She was stunning. He could find no other word that than that. Stunning. Stunned, literally something physical that struck his body when he looked at her, sitting there, serene but so, so certainly, sad.

What was it about this mystical lady that gave her a glimpse of tears? He took in every inch of her face, every crease of her blue velvet dress, as though somewhere, in some small piece of canvas, he could find the cause; find and rectify. But not in her face or her clothes, not in the elegant hands that reached out, fingers intertwined, across the bare walnut table, was there a hint or a clue.

Late into the night he would sit and look. Above him, his family slept: in front of him, she stayed forever awake. When the hour forced him to leave, it was with a sense of guilt that he crept away. She never ever left him: he left her, betrayed her each night and day, without ever coming close to rectifying the cause of her unhappiness. Went about his daily routine as though ordinary life was more important than the urgent, incestuous pulsing he felt.

In the early days he had been unsure. The canvas was big – too big for the room really, and possibly it dominated the space. But all who saw it never felt that it overpowered. Rather they invariably centred on the face which met their gazes, in the elegance and lineaments of the whole scene. So she stayed, held within the expensive, delicate frame that had housed her for almost a century.

Once, when he was about eight, he had seen the canvas in its previous setting. A well-to-do aunt in Ireland had entertained the family one summer for a holiday, and he remembered the picture looking down from the broad staircase that led to the wide landing at the top. "That's your great grandmother," his father had told him, "a very mysterious lady." But he never asked, and was never told, what was mysterious about her, and a falling out between his father and aunt had led to no more visits to the grand home. The picture faded into family history and was spoken about no longer. More than forty years later, it had come as a shock to be informed that the recently deceased aunt had bequeathed her long-estranged nephew twelve thousand pounds from her estate, some relatively valuable jewels, a rusting vintage car, and the picture.

It was his twin daughters who began leading him towards her. Unlike most adults, they found nothing attractive in the portrait. Instead, from an early age, they let it cultivate their fears, frightening themselves by insisting that the eyes followed them, wherever they went in the room. To the young, impressionable girls, the great-great grandmother was a source of alarm, not of beauty or fascination.

The superstitions amused him, though he agreed with his children on one point: the eyes did follow you. Wherever you stood or sat in the room, she looked at you. Looked through the dark, hazy eyes, drew your eyes back into them, in and through the pinpricks of light, until...

He went cold the first time he realized. And realization brought him to himself, laughing nervously at the moment which had just passed. Yet he looked again, and the smile, the laughter, melted like snow in fire. He whispered, 'Dear God', uncertain why he had said it, why only now he's staring into a face that he had seen, but never seen, before. In all the previous weeks, when he had displayed her and debated her, not once had he studied this face of which others has spoken about so freely.

She was stunning. Unbelievably, inexplicably lovely.

No, that wasn't it! He had seen more beautiful, more perfect women. His own wife for one. But in this face, in these eyes, lay something which overtook words like beauty and lovely and made them seem insipid. No words he had ever heard or uttered had done what was being done to him now, for he felt himself being drawn into the face, magnetized by it, compelled to begin a journey that he knew he should not make.

In these first moments of discovery an amalgam of sensations flooded him. Yet it was no trance, no relinquishing of the will. In a way that he found fascinating but frightening, he was able to observe and analyse exactly what was happening to him: the pulse in his chest strong and quick; the concentration of his eyes; the shallow breaths he was taking. All those sloppy teenage songs and poems about love taking your breath away – meaningless and cliché-ridden. Here it was.

He told no one, for there was no one to tell. Some of his colleagues at work had and were having affairs, kept a mistress, often with little attempt at secrecy, as though they did it by right, a sort of status symbol for the professional man. He had never approved, but had never judged them. In his eyes, a man made his own moral decisions and it was not up to others to interfere. He himself had sown a few wild oats in his teens whilst at university, but since his marriage he had been faithful to his wife – even if, he ruefully surmised, his own slightly overweight lack of physical attraction meant his chances to err were not that great. What he found in stable, married life was satisfaction enough for a person who had never wanted to climb the peaks of life, in either his personal or professional life. If others thought him staid and conventional, he thought their thirst for titillation a little pathetic. Perhaps if he had joined their ranks and taken under his private wing a young secretary willing to give him some thrills, he might have confided in someone there. Though this was different. It crossed, not the bounds of morality, but of sanity. You did not fall in love with a portrait.

His wife noticed nothing. For the length of his marriage he had never had to conjure up serious deceit, yet now, when it was needed, he found it strangely easy. Possibly because their love had been formal and unsurprising - a meeting of bodies and habits rather than minds - there had always been an unspoken distance between them. She had been less educated than he might have wished, a slightly surprising match to some of his university friends, but she had been pleasant, responsive and available. They had fulfilled each other's finite ambitions, had rarely disappointed each other, and had raised two healthy children who passed as successful and well bred. Each had an occupation which complemented their home life admirably, and so between them passed mostly what was polite and unembarrassing.

If this made it easier to keep the truth at distance, it also helped that he was good at it. The hours he spent in front of the picture were hours which extra work demanded. The look of distance, which was occasionally perceived, was the pondering of some problem he had brought home. It was all accepted as quite normal abnormality, taking its place amidst the statutory, repetitive conversation, the routine lovemaking, the sleeping and waking and eating and working.

Within him he held two ends of a day. Away from the portrait night was closing. There was light enough for this world, but day by day it grew dimmer, and the people who occupied it that much harder to distinguish. It was like writing in the half-light: he could go on with the mechanism, guessing the shapes of the letters and lines, but he could not look back to read what he had written. And soon would come complete dark.   But at night dawn broke.   Sitting and studying her, the light intensified, as in the other world it dimmed. The hours away from her became mere time to struggle through, but once with her he felt complete. He knew that he was obsessed; knew that to spend hour upon hour looking at her ought to have brought boredom; knew that his life, or perhaps only his mind, was drifting away from him. Yet knowing changed nothing.

He searched the face to find the reason for that slight, solitary tear. What is it? If the hands that rested on the table could be touched, reassured, he would have the story. If the body that sat proudly silent could be held and caressed, he would remedy it. What is it? The question possessed him more and more: the last thought at night; the first of his waking moments. The tear, the hint of sadness, the fingers, the body: what is it?

As the grey dawn filtered into the bedroom, his wife became conscious of her solitariness. Her husband's bed was empty, undisturbed. Reason began seeping into her mind. He was not away. Last night he was working downstairs. The faintest alarm sounded within her as she reached for the

clock and then her dressing-gown. He surely could not still
be working at five in the morning; or had he fallen asleep
over his papers?

The dining room was empty. All the downstairs rooms
were empty. The bathroom, the lavatories, the spare
bedroom, the attic, even the children's bedrooms were
checked before she returned to sit, disquieted, on her bed.

It took a few minutes to realise that she had not checked
in the garage. Now, with some degree of panic, she ran
downstairs, unbolted the front door, and oblivious of the
morning wind on her face and the wet concrete on her feet,
she pulled the iron handle of the garage door. Going back for
the keys, she mouthed an agnostic prayer against whatever
strangeness was enveloping her. Her hands fumbled the
awkward key, but eventually the door opened.

The red mini and the dark BMW seemed almost to greet
her. She flicked on the light and stood looking. Some residue
of reason made her feel the bonnets of both cars, cold as the
morning, and to look inside at their empty seats. Now,
without rushing, she switched off the light and wandered
back into the house.

The lights were on where she had left them in each
downstairs room, and she made no effort to turn them off.
The front door clicked shut smoothly and she walked slowly
into the kitchen, preoccupied and fearful, before the
impossible crashed into her brain and made her freeze.

She halted and looked stupidly at the front door. What
had she done three minutes ago? As though a victim of some
awful interrogation, she made herself silently answer:
unbolted the door. Unbolted the door.

Please, dear God, what was happening? She had unbolted
the door which she herself had locked on her way to bed,
having left her husband with the standard 'Get to bed soon'.

Immediately she raced to the back door in the kitchen: locked and bolted, the keys still hanging on the hook. Then to the French windows in the dining room, knowing that she would find that they too were secure. Unbelief and panic made her begin to cry, but still she went around the house to discover that everything was shut tight, every door and window locked or fastened from the inside. Once more she searched each room, desperate for this sick feeling to be resolved by simple discovery, for there to be some silly, rational cause, something she had forgotten and could laugh about, something only something to explain it. Eventually she had to wake the children to ask if they had let their father out of the house. She knew, of course, they hadn't.

In spite of a protracted, at times reluctant investigation, belief, unbelief, sympathy, suspicion and eventual cooling of official interest, no-one produced a single tangible idea. The police made efforts to establish that no one had seen the missing person, and all personal documents and credit cards remained in the house and so were not traceable. Nobody could account for the way the man had disappeared, but unless the wife had been lying, it simply remained a mystery, and an unfamed missing middle-aged man was not like a missing child. The detective in charge genuinely did not know what more could be done.

For the woman, the sense of loss was outweighed the weight of strangeness. Living without her husband was easier than living with his sudden disappearance. She was not a person to be devastated, but the logicality of it all, which she seemed to carry uniquely, weighed upon her.

Within five months the financial constraints of having two-thirds of an income missing began to bite. She could claim no life insurance without proof of death, yet the mortgage still needed payment. After another two months, the house was sold, many of the contents crammed into a three bedroom flat which barely held them. Certain items of furniture, too large for the new surroundings, were sold privately: the large oak dining table, the attic bookcase, the spare sofa and armchairs.

Only the picture remained when the house was bare. Far too big for the flat, nobody had volunteered to buy it, so she decided to leave it for the new owners to dispose of. It had no sentimental value for her: it was her husband's ancestry, not hers, and she felt no attachment to it. The children certainly were not keen to retain it.

She left the dining room for the final time, mindful of the last moment she had seen her husband in this very spot. She gave no more than a glimpse to the woman in blue velvet who now looked out over the bare space. As the door shut, the Victorian face was clouded in shadow, peering across the floating dust of the empty room, her expression serene, her eyes tearless, her hands gently reaching towards the three sturdy fingers, barely visible, on the far side of the bare table.

DRIVING AMBITION

"One of these days your impatience is going to be your downfall!"

Jimmy eased the black gear lever up to third and flicked the steering wheel lightly to fill the gap he had just created in the line of traffic. "No way mum, I know what I'm doing. You drive as fast as some of these old codgers and you end up getting nowhere." The red Polo picked up speed and then braked heavily as a bus in front slowed at a changing traffic light. Jimmy cursed, but quietly enough that his mother didn't catch it. He'd had enough lectures about his manners and his temper for one day. Regardless, the lecture went on. "I don't understand why you change so once you get behind the wheel. You're not like that in other ways."

"Brings out the real person in you, so they say," Jimmy smirked.

His mother puckered her lip and left it there. If the previous five hundred complaints had cut no ice with her son it was unlikely that this one would make any difference. But she did worry. So many young people seemed to have accidents from driving too fast. She'd read statistics to show how much more vulnerable they were than older drivers. Thank heaven only that Jimmy had never wanted a motorbike!

The letter was on the floor when Jimmy got home. The yell of delight brought his mother from the kitchen in some alarm. "What on earth is the matter?"

"Got an interview. Next Tuesday. Ricketts and Bloom!"

"Is that the one you wanted then?"

"Wanted! They're the top firm. And I'm going to be their top boy. Just wait and see, mum, just wait and see."

No ordinary job, and no ordinary chance. At twenty-six Jimmy was just beginning to have the first spasms of panic about his future career. Personnel manager in the small company he worked for was not a bad position, but it wasn't Jimmy's ceiling. Now, Ricketts and Bloom was another world, another universe! Status, pay increase, openings for the big, big world of the City.... the world his oyster! Three hundred pounds on a new suit, ninety on new designer shoes and seventy-five on a very chic satin tie was the least that Jimmy could allow himself. All would be more than covered by the pay increase from his first month's salary.

Jimmy's self-confidence alone might have been enough to convince him that success was assured. He was, after all, good at his job, had made his way up the ladder within a couple of years of joining his present firm and had attracted the attention of the managing director on more than a few occasions. Not once had he blotted his copybook; not a blemish on a steady, if so far short, career in the field of dealing with people.

But added to that was Elaine Arden.

Jimmy had met Elaine at a function some two months previous, a rather tedious affair which both had attended out of duty. An attraction of mutual boredom could have been the impetus for their talking, but it led quickly to shop talk, a revealing of professional positions and another meeting three days later at which Elaine had broached the idea of Jimmy working for her company: Ricketts and Bloom. The vaguest hint of attraction had entered Jimmy's mind upon their first meeting, but the suggestion of Elaine being a door through which he might advance his career suddenly painted her in a new and more appealing light. OK, so she wasn't exactly his ideal type: dark-haired, rather skinny and a little plain. But nonetheless, not without attraction; not embarrassing to be with in a pub full of his friends. It was not love for life, of that Jimmy was certain, but equally he was convinced that he was not just using her for a foothold into the firm. Any ending of the friendship would be mutual.

Elaine had given no assurances. At the moment there were no openings in the firm, but turnover tended to be quite high and there was a good chance that a position might soon come along. Moreover, as Deputy Head of Personnel, Elaine had the ear and the confidence of her boss, a rather old-fashioned Scotsman with a sharp tongue that he used with everyone except Elaine. "He fancies you," had been Jimmy's conclusion, to which she laughed but did not demur.

The opening came quicker than either of them had expected. Mr. Hope, her boss, had summarily sacked one of his leading under-managers for having the temerity to argue back, perhaps a little too vehemently. Ignoring the threats of action for unfair dismissal and industrial tribunals, Hope had personally cleared out his junior's desk and dispatched him within an hour. An hour later Elaine telephoned Jimmy to suggest he had a CV ready and waiting.

The same evening Jimmy took Elaine to a country club where they dined, the meal being preceded and followed by the most frightening car rides she had ever undertaken.

Jimmy was aware of her terror, but considered that no real risk was being taken. A car made to drive matched to a young man with excellent reflexes presented no real danger in his eyes; and it would be something she would remember, something she could talk about to her friends in the years to come.

Elaine assured Jimmy that at the earliest opportunity she would tell her boss about him. Mr. Hope seemed to be in no hurry to find a replacement, but Elaine was confident that he would listen to her in a positive way. She would also point out to him the advantage of filling the position through word of mouth rather than going to the time and expense of advertising. "That should appeal to his Scottish nature," she laughed. Jimmy bought her another vodka.

It took, in fact, ten days for Mr. Hope to act. Elaine had initially mentioned Jimmy as someone she had heard about who had been recommended, then had handed her boss his CV, a very impressive and professional document, then discussed its contents with him, managing to adopt an impressed tone in her voice without sounding unduly enthusiastic. No mention of personal acquaintance. Not a hint of bias. Purely professional judgement.

Her boss had then sat on it. Much to Jimmy's frustration and Elaine's fears, he had said no more about the idea, and Elaine had been unwilling to pursue it for fear of an adverse reaction. Without saying another word to her, however, he instructed his secretary to invite the young man for a meeting on the following Tuesday.

"Whatever you do, be respectful. Make sure you call him 'sir'. He thinks working in Personnel you should ooze charm twenty four hours a day."

"But I do," laughed Jimmy. "I won't utter a word out of place."

"I'm sure it'll be alright. He's not seeing anyone else about the job, so it's all in your hands."

"Don't worry, I'll impress him from the word go."

Jimmy looked admiringly in the mirror at the cut of his new suit. The tie couldn't have matched more perfectly: the exact blend of professionalism and elegance.

The drive to Ricketts and Bloom would take only twenty-five minutes, but Jimmy decided to leave an hour so that he could familiarise himself with the building and its surroundings. The odd word in an interview to show that he was au-fait with the Company wouldn't come amiss. Besides, punctuality had always been one of his hallmarks: not late once in six years of work.

As usual, his driving demonstrated anything other than that he had time to spare. Belted and cocooned into his special space, with instruments in front of him giving every ounce of information from the time to his speed to the temperature, he set off with customary aggression, practising some of the phrases that he would attempt to use in his interview later that morning. He was still in the Ricketts office as he cut sharply in front of a dark Land Rover, but then had to screech to a halt to avoid a teenage girl at a crossing. The girl looked momentarily terrified, whilst the car behind blasted its horn at the near-accident. At the next set of lights it drew alongside Jimmy. A grey-haired woman and a man with a ridiculous yellow bow tie, which made Jimmy instantly, laugh, glared across at him, the man clearly mouthing his anger. As the lights changed, Jimmy gave the staring driver an emphatic V-sign and yelled "Pratt!" before screeching off along the dual carriageway.

Five minutes later, the blue light of a police car reared up in his interior mirror. Pulling over to the inside lane and slowing down to let the vehicle go past, Jimmy's heart sank as it passed him, and then signalled for him to stop. This was not in the script! An officer, about the same age as Jimmy, approached the car. For a moment Jimmy visualised this same young man out of uniform and out of the police force, sitting opposite him being interviewed for a job at Ricketts. Boot on the other foot then, my son! The officer's voice broke the reverie. The customary, "Is this your car, sir?" Answer politely; don't antagonise; play the obsequious repentant; get away quickly! "Yes officer, is there a problem?"

We had a report a few minutes ago about this vehicle being driven recklessly, dangerously." Bow tie! Damn him! "Are you aware that you've been causing concern with your driving sir?"

"Err, no officer. In fact I'm quite surprised. I'm a very careful driver – see, my license is clean." Jimmy handed over his documents. Good card to play. Just please don't take all day looking at them. The officer handed them back as the second policeman arrived.

"Registered to a James Burton, Elmer Road." The first officer nodded, gave a glance up and down the car and then spoke again to Jimmy. "Nice car sir. Keep it that way. And don't go upsetting other drivers." Jimmy nodded. A mutual understanding of guilt without proof passed between the three young men and the policemen returned to their vehicles.

Jimmy eased the car into a steady second gear, following behind the police car at a respectable distance and speed.

Could have been awkward! Could have made him late! Lucky day, so don't push the luck too far. Without once breaking the speed limit, Jimmy turned into Ricketts' private car park ten minutes later, still a quarter of an hour before his set interview time.

The receptionist telephoned through his arrival and Elaine appeared a minute later. In the lift up he briefly told her about his escapade with the police, but she more urgently told him that if he could somehow mention his liking of fishing, this, she had remembered, was one of Mr. Hope's passions and might well prove a useful aide. Jimmy quickly absorbed the news. Fishing wasn't his forte, but he could bluff his way around salmon and trout if he had to, he was sure of that.

Elaine showed him into a waiting room, bedecked with prints of Scottish scenes all round the wall. "He's got someone with him at the moment, but I'll take you in as soon as he's finished. Have a seat." Instead, Jimmy looked from one print to another, thinking of what intelligent remarks he might make about fly fishing and bait. The door opened and a young woman walked out of the waiting room carrying an armful of files. A minute later Elaine came out. "Mr. Hope can see you now," she announced in a clear voice, mouthing the words "Good luck" as her back was turned to the office door. Jimmy smiled his thanks and walked through the door.

Mr. Hope rose and held out a hand towards the newcomer. Jimmy's hand set out in reply, but in a moment frozen for all time, it remained a career span away from contact. Frozen too, were the two sets of eyes that connected, the one pair above the expensive silk tie that matched so perfectly with the expensive designer suit; the other pair, above a less modern three piece suit, grey, pin-striped, conservative, prevented from being completely boring only by the outrageous, but now less hysterical, yellow bow tie of its wearer.

SNAKES AND LADDERS

I'd been at Mountsfield School for almost nine years when Julia Boswell arrived to take over the art department. Small, suave and elegant, I was struck by her confidence at our very first meeting. Gerald Green, the Head, introduced me as I passed them in the corridor: "Oh, Fiona, this is Julia Boswell who has just been appointed Head of Art. Julia, Fiona Dalby, one of our longer-serving stalwarts. Fiona's in charge of our pastoral policy."

The quick reply, in a firm Yorkshire accent, wasn't instantly appealing: "Good, I'll know who to come to about poor discipline then." I caught the Head's eye for a split second - long enough to detect an amused twinkle. You didn't need to work in the school for the years I had to appreciate what a poor judge of character Gerald Green was, and how easily he fell prey to certain of the female staff who won concessions from him with little more than a pretty, youthful smile. I judged that he had also become an instant fan of North Country bluntness.

Julia quickly made her mark in the school. It became clear that she was straight out of the top drawer for educational jargon, and wasted no time in changing as much as she could, both within her own department and throughout the school. There was no missing the Art room with its new look – more like a garden centre than a school classroom, with pots crowding every corner of the room.

But her dealings with children was the area that caused

irritation. On the one hand there was immense liberalism that other teachers found disturbing. In her lessons it was nothing unusual to see uniforms discarded and pupils with food on their desks and stereos in their ears, sometimes lounging around in the newly imported armchair, producing, so it seemed, some very odd-looking designs or paintings or clay models. The familiarity extended to Julia making comments about other staff within pupils' earshot, though never more than a double-entendre that made complaints hard to substantiate.

It might be assumed that such a regime would have endeared Julia to impressionable youngsters, but the reverse was the case. She managed to cause one confrontation after another, often with well-motivated and enthusiastic students. Her sharp tongue always scored a victory over less-experienced youngsters, but I found no satisfaction in picking up the pieces, trying to placate wronged pupils without sounding disloyal to a colleague. The result was that after the initial euphoria of unconventional freedom in art lessons, many children took a strong dislike to her.

A lot of staff, too, never warmed. We were a close-knit community, but not one that excluded newcomers. Julia made little attempt to establish friendships, but she wasn't averse to making pronouncements on political correctness or advocating all the latest 'isms' that found favour with the trendsetters. Early on I remember judging the temperature when commenting on theartistic talent of a fourteen year-old boy who had produced an excellent still-life drawing. I was lectured by Julia that there was no such thing as 'talent' and that it merely depended on the opportunity that each child was given to flourish. I chose not to argue, only to give Julia as wide a berth as I could.

I think if Julia had had a sense of humour, or perhaps a less acerbic tongue, she might have been better liked. But she had the narrow-mindedness of a political extremist, unable to step back and look at herself, unwilling to concede that there might just be flaws in some of her ideas. The qualities of forcefulness that she did possess, whilst winning her few friends perhaps, had certainly enabled her to rise quickly to a head of department within her profession. Coming late into teaching after a decade in advertising, she had spent only three years to reach her present position. Whatever else she lacked, she had the gift of the gab.

A year after Julia came, Pat Anderson, the deputy head, took early retirement. I'd always got on well with Pat, and she told me the news before it became public. "Make sure you put in for the job, Fiona. You'll stand a really good chance"

My mind began to race. Somewhere inside me I knew that a deputy headship would be my next possible move, but being happy in my job, it had all seemed so remote as not to consider seriously. Now here it was, within my sights: a job I knew I could do, and do well.

Both at school and at home I received further encouragement. Graham was certain that I should go for it, and the twins, just coming up to ten, thought it mightbe cool for their image to have a mother who was a deputy at a secondary school. I found it all reassuring, but I'd already made up my mind to apply. I argued with Graham against my hopes: "There'll be a lot of applicants, you know, once they advertise it nationally. I may not even get short listed."

"Of course you will. Good internal candidate – you start off with an advantage."

"Suppose they don't want an internal candidate? Suppose they want fresh blood?"

"Well you'll just have to see, won't you. But I reckon you'll get it."

I heard on the grapevine – the most reliable grapevine being Audrey the school secretary – that there had been sixty-three applications. More than that she could not or would not say, and so it was with strict formality that I received a letter through the door informing me that I had, indeed, been short listed for the post, and asking me to attend for an interview the following Monday. I had to admit to myself that it wasn't totally unexpected; nevertheless, it brought a surge of relief. Out of sixty-three, I was down to a final few.

Audrey had no qualms in telling me that she knew all along that I would be interviewed, and from her I gained the information that there would be five other candidates the following week: two women from local schools, one of whom I used to work with; one woman coming up from Cornwall; a man, whom Audrey smilingly dismissed as the token male; and one other candidate: Julia Boswell.

I spent the week in a pretence of normality. In my conversations both at school and at home I shunned serious talk of my prospects for success, yet inside I regularly failed to control my imagination. My rational voice told a fanciful mind not to play games of taking up residence in the deputy head's office, not to organize my first term's work, deciding my new priorities, my philosophy, my shifting relationship with the Head. I was a candidate, not the heir apparent. But the voice of sense had little chance against the thoughts which flew in at any unguarded moment.

Equally useless were attempts to try to control the fits of confidence and depression which blew like the wind. One moment might bring a surge of optimism as I saw myself the obvious choice for the job, almost invincible considering I was being interviewed by people, many of whom I knew. Then the gauge would plummet as I thought of other candidates, what extra skills or experience they might have to offer, and perhaps how limited and inadequate I could appear on the day.

As a touch of compensation I read up on a few articles and documents that Pat suggested, mainly things I already knew, and browsed through a couple of books on educational management which she had lent me. But it all felt a bit false, and though I decided to absorb a few details, I resolved that I would just try to be myself on the day, and not a mere answer machine churning out the latest in acceptable philosophy. Besides, I reasoned, the more I read, the more I became aware of how little I really knew: hence the greater opportunity for nervousness.

When the day actually arrived I found the twins and Graham excited beyond anything I felt. Driving into school had a strangeness about it, for today I was not Mrs. Dalby, going straight to her registration class, but a prospective deputy head teacher, going through the formalities of reporting to the secretary and then being ushered into the Head's office to join the other candidates.

It was a day-long affair, with written exercises, individual interviews, then lunch followed by half-hour sessions with ten of the governors. This last part was the most gruelling, I felt, for whilst there were familiar faces around the table there were also awkward questions from an inspector whom I had not encountered. At least it seemed to pass quickly, and by four o'clock the five of us were waiting together in the Head's office for the announcement.

I had had time during the day to form impressions of the others, and thereby what I thought of their respective chances – and threats to me. The man seemed a genuine no-hoper, very nervous and apparently quite inexperienced. I wondered how much truth there had been in Audrey's throw-away description. I gave him little chance, especially as the retiring deputy was a woman. My former colleague had changed since I last saw her and now seemed much more positive and confident. I felt she was in with a shout, but not as much as the lady from Cornwall who seemed every bit a deputy head. She had, in fact, been acting as deputy in her own school for the past three months. I reckoned on her as my greatest rival, and a part of me was already considering how I would work under her if she were appointed. As for Julia, she had been reserved to the point of rudeness during the day, choosing not to talk with the other candidates more than she had to. I put it down to nervousness. I doubt the others were so generous in their judgement. Watching her now, she lit one cigarette after another whilst the rest of us engaged in conversation to quell our own nerves.

At ten to five exactly the door opened. The appointed governor uttered half a dozen incredible, shattering words: "Could we see Mrs. Boswell please."

She was up and out in a flash, the door closing on eight eyes expressing silent, appalled disbelief. I had never experienced such an instant let-down in my life : three weeks of conscious and unconscious expectation exploded like a burst balloon, and with just about the same speed.

"I just can't believe it. How could they possibly appoint her? How?"

"Because she probably charmed them with all the latest jargon", Graham replied, barely disguising the bitterness he too felt

"How can they be so gullible? It's just like the blind leading the blind."

"No it's not, it's the stupid appointing the stupid." Graham's voice resonated now with genuine and uncharacteristic anger. If anything, he felt more angry than I did. "It happens all the time. People who know nothing about real education appoint idiots to top positions. Just look around and see how many lunatic heads there are in this area. Look at your bloke! Andgood sensible teachers get trodden on or ignored."

I felt too angry to cry. Disappointment was only part of the package, what I would have felt if the Cornwall woman or my ex-colleague had landed the job. At least then I would have had some understanding of the decision. But not this: this was just incomprehensible.

Graham's voice penetrated again. "She'll be up at the top within five years. Head first, then inspector, then who knows what. She'll slither and slide her way right p the ladder. You watch."

The remaining few weeks of the term were incredibly difficult, despite the kindness, the support and the expressed indignation which came from many quarters. My feelings were terribly confused, a mixture off anger and resentment and sadness and self-pity too. I thought of resigning but decided against it. I'd be cutting off my nose in doing so, as well as leaving a job I actually liked. Nevertheless, I wanted somehow to express my rage, to make some protest against being, as I thought, discarded.

At the same time I realized that my response belonged more to the realms of the adolescents that I taught than to a supposedly mature adult. (How often, I reflected, did teachers behave worse than their pupils). Sulking was easy: made easier by people's sympathy. I determined that I had to grow up, to grow out of it, but it was easier said than done.

Julia, meanwhile, practiced her new role with the smoothness of an engine without oil. What battles were going to lie ahead next term when the mantle was fully donned! Yet, like teachers often do, everyone seemed to acquiesce and avoid blow-ups. How more honest the children were on this score. They often spoke their minds and damned the consequences whilst we bit our tongues out of impotence or self-preservation.

One ludicrous result of this was that the traditional end-of year staff barbeque somehow found itself sited at the Boswell's residence. I gathered it was meant to be a kind of public celebration for her sudden elevation, though I could find no-one who thought it was a good venue or understood just how it had been hijacked. Graham was adamant that I shouldn't go, but I argued with him and myself that my absence would seem churlish and petty, and that for my own self-esteem I had to attend. He remained unconvinced. "Well don't expect me to go this year, because I'm not. I'd almost certainly be incredibly rude to the woman and to your idiot headmaster for having her appointed."

As a concession to Graham's indignation I left late for the party, but he still managed to convey his disapproval. "Well, *we're* going to have an evening of fun and games, aren't we kids!" The dramatic effect was slightly spoiled by the twins arguing over which game they were going to play, and Graham and I shared a self-conscious smile, both feeling a modicum of guilt over our actions.

I arrived at half-past nine for a barbeque that had started at seven. Amid the regular faces were a few new and unfamiliar ones, partners of the more recent members of staff. Julia greeted me with uncharacteristic gaiety, pointing me to the abundant food and drink. The evening had turned chilly and many people had moved from the garden inside. I wasted no time in getting away from Julia and squeezed through bodies to get into the narrow kitchen. Here, a large, balding man whom I didn't know, seemed to have adopted the role of bartender. "Ah, a new-comer I perceive," he said, rather too loudly. "And what can I get for the beautiful little lady?" I felt the hairs of dislike bristle on my head, but my answer was civil enough not to show. The drink was accompanied by a smile so smarmy that I wondered if it was meant to be a deliberate joke that I wasn't getting. I caught Pat's eye in the doorway and realized she was guessing my thoughts.

Outside on the patio I was about to ask her the identity of Prince charming when the answer preceded the question. "That, darling, is Adrian, Julia's beloved. Well matched, don't you think?"

As the evening progressed, Adrian's presence became oppressive. The loud laughter sounded more false with each bellow; the swearing became stronger and more audible. Worst of all was the way he kept touching some of the younger women – not indecently, but still, with the draped arm around the shoulder, unpleasant enough to cause offence. I half suspected it would finish in a scene, but then, quite suddenly, he seemed to have disappeared from the ensemble. So, I noticed, had a rather good-looking and flirtatious young student teacher who had arrived at the party after me.

By midnight I'd had enough. The party gave little sign of breaking up, but I felt I'd done my duty. I wandered back into the hot, stuffy kitchen, full of smoke, the smell of stale beer and the rather too loud sound ofElton John competing with music from another room in the house. In the sitting room there were still people dancing and I motioned my good-byes to a few, looking for Frances to offer the formalities.

I couldn't see her anywhere and thought she must have gone back into the garden. It was only as I went upstairs to get my jacket that I noticed her, leaning crookedly against one of the bedroom doors, a glass in one hand and a cigarette in the other, the make up on her face smudged and blotchy by the tears that ran down it. The sight of her crying instinctively took me towards her, but she seemed oblivious of who I was: merely that I was someone. Clearly very drunk, she mouthed some obscenities about her husband, and burst into more noisy crying. I quickly sensed that neither an excess of alcohol, nor her husband's philandering, were novel events in her life.

She looked as pathetic as anyone I had ever seen and I felt sad for her without really feeling sympathy. This was her alternative life. When she left her empire at school, this was what she had to come home to. Some alternative.

It made a difference as I drove home. It seemed awful at the time that I somehow felt good, but my bitterness was gone. I knew what I was going home to, and knew that no ambition would make me exchange it for what Julia had.
I crept Into a sleeping house, woke Graham unfairly with a hard kiss, then tiptoed into the twins' bedroom to see them sleeping. The room was its usual mess and I felt stupidly reassured. Picking up the board game that littered the floor, I laid it on the desk, glimpsing in the light from the landing

outside the long ladder that went from 18 up to 65, and the smiling snake that slipped from the very top line down to deep, disappointing obscurity.

WEDDING RECEPTION

The service had lived up to the limited expectations of all who had possessed expectations. The weather had remained kind insofar as, if the sun had not quite shone, the rain had decided to avoid spoiling the photographs in the vestry gardens. The church was two-thirds full, comprising the traditional blend of family, friends and work colleagues, all combining heartily to sing none of the chosen hymns. The bride, plainness disguised as much as possible, had her wish fulfilled of walking down the aisle in her white wedding gown to traditional organ music, and the vicar, a pallid and weasel-looking individual, had not minded in the least that neither she nor groom professed the slightest faith or interest in what his church was meant to stand for.

The couple's drive to the hotel was suitably ostentatious in an open carriage pulled by two shiny black horses. Noticed they wanted to be, and noticed they were, at least if the hoots of passing motorists were any yardstick. Upon arrival, a dapper little man with brylcreemed hair took charge of proceedings, ushering the pair into the hotel reception room where they were to greet the incoming guests.

Fifty minutes later, they were seated for the wedding meal, a hearty offering of pork, potatoes and overcooked vegetables, which managed to draw generous if undeserving, praise from many of the assembled. After the sweet, coffee and a suitable pause, Brylcreem prayed silence for the first of the speeches.

The bride's father was a man of unexceptional ability in numerous fields. If he were to compile a CV it would be based around his life spent at the local working men's club where he was known as a member. In his whole life since leaving school at the age of sixteen, he had been called upon only once to speak publicly, and that was to thank friends for attending his surprise fiftieth birthday celebration, which he had known about for weeks. A man of limited words and limited ideas, speaking now was an ordeal that ought to have phased him at least slightly. Instead, however, he appeared to revel in the opportunity, unaware of the incoherent nonsense that was emanating from his mouth. But such is the spirit of generosity that surrounds these occasions, he was given hearty applause when his listeners guessed he was making a joke, and a rapturous ovation when at last he finished.

Much to the consternation of the dapper master of ceremonies, tradition was now dispensed with as, instead of the groom speaking next, it befell his best man to make his long prepared speech. The new husband, seemingly, had requested this reversal of positions, believing, as he stated, that it should be the groom who had the last word on such an occasion. No one appeared unduly bothered.

The best man rose to admiring glances from the two young impressionable bridesmaids. Suave, good-looking and immensely aware of his attributes, he had looked forward to this opportunity for some weeks. Now, armed with a scroll of jokes, witticisms and stories, he began his performance.

"I'd like to begin this speech by saying to Darren that he couldn't have made a better choice for a partner than Sandra. And Sandra, you couldn't have made a worse one."

On cue, the gathered assembly laughed and applauded as if they had never heard the joke before. Buoyed by such an impressive response, the speaker moved up a gear, relating first, a history of how he had met his good friend four years ago whilst playing in the local pub football team, then outlining some of the amusing idiosyncrasies he had noticed about him, including his tendency to vomit after too many beers, and going on to retell jokes about marriage that he had found in The Bumper Book of Funny Stories. After ten minutes of undiluted success, with one bridesmaid ready to offer herself as his sacrificial virgin, the best man sat down to the congratulations of those around him, almost matching the ones he offered himself.

Following his best man, Darren cut an instantly less impressive figure. A very slightly receding hairline gave an impression of more years than he owned, whilst his indulgence for food and drink had left a stomach barely contained by the light blue suit he sported. A more perceptive judge, however, might have concluded that he carried none of the swagger or conceit of the previous speaker, and though his opening remarks were delivered more quietly, they were more genuine.

"I'd like to thank you all for coming today. I hope you have had a good meal, and I'm sure you'll remember today for a long time." Stifled smiles were held in check at the awkward phraseology, but unaware or undeterred, Darren continued to thank and compliment the bridesmaids and other various helpers who had done such a splendid and difficult job in handing out hymn books in church. The listeners waited expectantly for a light-hearted remark, but it remained closeted. Darren continued his homily:

"I'd especially like to thank Mr and Mrs Willoughby for providing such a nice hotel for this reception. I'm glad it was providing such a nice hotel for this reception. I'm glad it was rather expensive." The masses waited for the punch line, which never followed. One or two fidgeted with slight embarrassment; Darren looked down at his notes. A wise head in the room decided it would be politic to applaud the aforementioned parents in the light of no follow-up.

Shaking slightly, the groom picked up his speech again. "As you will know, there are very many people who are involved in the preparation of a wedding, and if I haven't mentioned you by name then I'm sorry and please accept my thanks." He paused to look down again, then glanced at his new wife, smiled timidly, and went on. "There are two people, though, who really need to be singled out more than any other."

Warming anticipation from his hearers. "And they are, of course, my best man, Steve, and my wife Sandra." As friends and relatives began to applaud once more, with a couple adding cheers, Darren caught the eye of both. Sandra smiled coyly and looked a little embarrassed. Steve smiled broadly and raised his champagne glass in response to the thanks. Before Darren got up and walked out of the reception, he added: "And I'd like to thank them for sleeping together for the past three months, and wish them good luck in the future."

ONE LAST TIME

Billy Pincher leaned across the table and squeezed Joyce's hand. He wanted her to look at him but she kept her face down, the tears rolling across her powdered cheek and onto to her bare forearm. She pulled her hand away and pushed the half-empty teacup across the table.

"It's alright Joyce love. It's alright." He paused for her to say something, but when she didn't he went on more quietly. "We've known this was going to happen, sometime. Always a probability."

"It's not alright. Don't say it is coz' it isn't. It's not alright and it's not gonna be alright."

Her voice was uncharacteristically petulant and Billy felt unsure how to respond. He paused for a moment and then walked to the window. Outside in the narrow cobbled street there was already an unusual bustle of people, neighbours from up and down the road who seemed content just to walk and stop and talk to anyone who was around. Even from inside the small front room with its thick curtains and rolled black-out, the sense of excitement was tangible, though for the two occupants of the house it was silence that permeated their minds.

Billy came back and sat again at the table where Joyce had remained motionless. He felt inadequate in this situation, but he finally made himself speak. "Joyce, it's best

I go love. Now that it's over, well, Jimmy could be back within a matter of days. I read that they've already released hundreds from some camps. He could already be on his way."

A noisy sob came from deep within Joyce's throat but Billy had to go on. "It wouldn't be fair for me to be here. You know we've talked about it dozens of times. After all this time Jimmy doesn't deserve this."

"I don't want you to go. I want you to stay here!"

"And I want to stay. Believe me, I'd give a million quid to stay. But I can't. And we both know it."

It was true, and in previous times, when the ending of the war was still only a distant, future event, they had both talked about this day: about how stoical, how brave they would be, and how when Jimmy came back home after four years in a Prisoner-of-War camp Joyce would forever fold away in some secret corner of her heart the love she had found with Billy and resume her life with the man she had married and lived with for only a few weeks of her life.

Billy's sense of right and fairness had been one of the things that had made Joyce love him so. It had taken him a long time to ever acknowledge the illicit love that had sprung up between them three years since, and for weeks he had fought against letting the relationship develop. Eventually it had become too strong, and too obvious to him that what he was feeling for Joyce was being felt by her in return. In the local park, on a warm and balmy Tuesday afternoon in September, he had warned her against his love, only to find her fingers intertwined in his and a shocking, first kiss taking place between them.

It had not taken long to become lovers, but Billy's sense of guilt at what he was doing took longer to evaporate. In the long dark hours of the night he would tell Joyce that he could never take Jimmy's place, that she must never expect him to do so. He related to her again and again how Jimmy had risked and eventually forfeited his own freedom so that he, Billy, badly wounded and in danger of dying, could be returned to his own lines and homeland. And only the insanely strong and passionate love he had developed for his mate's wife outweighed the waves of disgust that swept over him with regularity.

"You know we can't be together when he comes back. It's just too wrong, too wrong. As much as I love you Joyce, and God knows that I do, we can't hurt him in that way. He don't deserve it. You couldn't hurt him like that and neither could I."

Wrapped in each other's bodies the words had had no life of their own. When it happened, in some future far-off day, their feelings, their passion and longing, would be different, and they would cope, knowing they were doing the right thing. Such was the logic of their love. "We may not be doing what we should," Billy had told her, "and I can't pretend that it is right. But our love mustn't ever hurt anyone else, even if it hurts us."

"How can love hurt people?" Joyce had chided. "I always thought that love was the thing that brought you happiness. Isn't that what you grow up believing, what everyone tells you?"

"Sometimes love's not enough though, is it. Sometimes there's other things stronger, more important."

For the first time in minutes Joyce became aware of the activity outside the window. She got up from the table and looked through the net curtains. Her voice was calm, resigned, but she didn't turn and continued to gaze out of the window. The laughing faces of the people on the outside made her look just at the window pane.

"What will you do Billy?"

Billy's nails dug deeply into the palm of his hands. "I'm going away. It's best I go." He paused. "I'm going tonight."

Joyce turned suddenly with fearful eyes. "Why? Why so suddenly?"

"It's best I do. We don't know how soon he'll be back. It's best I go tonight."

"Where will you go?" Her voice strained to finish the sentence.

"I don't know yet. But Joyce love, it must be a proper break. It's got to be a goodbye, not a good night. I thought I might eventually go abroad. Maybe Canada."

For more than a minute neither of them spoke. The noises outside of laughter and celebration at the victory news seemed to taunt them in their misery. Finally Joyce asked, "Will you write? Will you let me know where you are?"

"It's best I don't. At least, not for a long time. A long, long time". Joyce leaned forward with her face on the pane and sobbed as Billy went on. "I know it seems hard and cruel, but if I go now, this morning, it'll be easiest for us. Believe me love."

Before he left, Billy held Joyce close to him in a long tight embrace. Leaving her was the hardest thing he had ever done in his life and no words, no actions, could begin to communicate the depth of his unhappiness. For her part, Joyce allowed herself to be hugged, but sobs wracked through her and she began to cry openly. The only words that were finally exchanged were a quiet "Goodbye Joyce. I'll always love you," and then Billy was gone.

For almost an hour Joyce slumped at the table, wanting to do nothing but cry out her despair, oblivious to the increasing bustle outside, to the late post coming through the door, to the noise of the neighbour's wireless blaring through the thin dividing wall of the houses.

A knocking at the door made her stir and without trying to disguise her red and bleary eyes she turned the lock and let in her mother. The older woman entered without a word, scooped up the three letters that lay on the floor and sat herself firmly in the corner armchair, removing the headscarf which she wore. A large barrel of a woman, her hard face lacked any attraction whatever. Joyce had always wondered how anyone could have found such a character lovable enough to marry, and as a mother she had poured out the minimum of affection on her two children. She looked now at her daughter without a hint of sympathy and her voice, when she finally spoke, was harsh and grating.

"So, it's finally happened. Like I told you it would. Like I told you all along".

Joyce made no reply but began busying herself washing the teacups in a bowl of water. "I suppose you're satisfied now," her mother continued. "And do you really think he's not going to find out? Do you suppose one of these nosy old crows along here won't tell him at the first opportunity?"

"I don't want to talk mum. Just leave me alone."

"He's gone I hope. And bloody good riddance too. I tell you girl, you've got a lot of clearing up to do before this mess is sorted out. Thank God your father isn't around to see it. He'd have choked the life out of that bugger. I don't know how you could have -"

"Mum!" Joyce grabbed her jacket and was in the street before her mother could utter a further word. There were people milling around at the doors to houses, a group of women standing in the middle of the road laughing, an old man balancing precariously on a chair trying to attach some bunting to his front window pane. The street was pregnant with expectation, save for the one figure that bustled purposefully along, head down, avoiding the familiar faces and the looks on them that she knew they would house.

It was a good twenty minutes walk to Billy's lodgings and by the time Joyce reached there she was panting and nauseous. But the walk had allowed her mind to clear and there was no hesitation in knocking firmly at the door. Immediately there were sounds from inside and the door opened quickly. Joyce's pulse began to race, expecting to see Billy, but it was the face of a woman she vaguely recognised that confronted her. Before she could recall the woman's name, came the urgent demand: "Where's Billy?"

The woman revealed the faintest of smirks before replying. "He's gone. Left this morning". She looked intently at Joyce to gauge the reaction.

"Where? Did he leave his address? He must have left a forwarding address."

"Not with me, Mrs. Parks". The last two words were almost spat out and only a fool would have failed to understand the contempt they carried.

Joyce remembered the woman, Billy's landlady from the next door house, as someone she had seen once before and who had on that solitary occasion displayed her feelings at the illicit relationship her tenant was having. But there was a more urgent and important issue now for the young woman to worry about. "You must have some idea. He must have told you something."

"Well he didn't, and there's an end on it. Now I've got this place to clean so if you'll excuse me..."

The door closed but Joyce remained still, as though believing it would open again to reveal the face she so desired.   Eventually she turned and shuffled slowly back towards her own house.

Her mother had gone but the smell of her cigarettes filled the small room. Joyce flopped into the armchair where her mother had been sitting and threw the lipstick coated dog end into the grate. She felt drained: too empty to cry any more, too exhausted to do anything other than sit stupidly and look at the tidy little room which had witnessed the most tearing separation of her life just a few hours before. She leaned back against the frayed, patterned back of the chair, closed her eyes and dozed fitfully.

When she woke properly the room was in semi-darkness. The young woman lifted herself and automatically went to close the blackout curtain before realising that now, that was a thing of the past. Things, from today, were different. But not just some things. Everything was different.

She took the three letters which her mother had placed on the table and began distractedly to open them. For the first time in the day she let her mind dwell on her husband - the man she had known for such a little while before his incarceration; the young boy who had begged her to marry him after six weeks of courtship; the innocent who had spent but two nights with her as her spouse before being shipped out to Africa.   What would four years of prison have done to him? Would she even know, let alone have feelings for, this comet who had shot impressively across her sky before disappearing? The one thing which was certain was that she could not love him: not in any sense of the word that she had used with Billy.

She threw down a letter from her young sister in Wales without reading it and allowed Billy into her mind once more. The ache was tangible. Joyce was not good at expressing herself in clever ways, but the image of a heavy, thick blanket across her life was so powerful that she felt she could cover herself with it. A future without Billy was a future of stifling monotony, a weight laid on her, which she was not capable of bearing. And to have no hope of contact with him, no idea of his whereabouts, no means to tell him secretly that she loved and longed for him, even as another man's wife.

Involuntarily she whispered his name, again and again. "Billy, oh Billy, Billy."

The letter she held was type-written and she took in an official seal at the top before anything else. The light was dim but good enough to show her the opening sentence. One by one important words arrowed into her: regret... your husband...191115 Corporal James Parks...injured in accident...died of injuries...northern German border...

Joyce collapsed into the armchair to absorb the letter completely. She felt the knocking of her heart against her ribs, as she comprehended its contents and then an uncanny calm, as she understood the implications. For a dreadful moment she feared she might laugh; then a wave of natural compassion swept her as she saw the youthful face of her boy husband. Almost instantly came the sudden thought that she was a widow; and only then did that suffocating curtain lift to allow her a path somewhere into the future.

The illogicality of shock gripped her for several moments as, rising from the chair, she mentally rushed to tell Billy the dreadful, liberating news. And then fell back again. The blanket returned, this time folded double by Billy. Billy, who had packed his belongings and left his digs that morning;

who had said that a clean break would be best, and had left no forwarding address; who could be heading now for any corner of the world. Billy, who had gone.

A torrent of thoughts now filled her mind. Should she return to Billy's digs and demand that his landlady tell her something of his whereabouts? Should she rush down now to the train station, in the hope that he would be there? Or what - or what? Even in the desperate state that now overtook her, nothing seemed a worthwhile avenue. Billy had no family home that she could contact; had not been able to work since being wounded; and she knew of no friends he had in the neighbourhood who might be able to tell her of him. In the time they had spent together they had been totally self-sufficient and by implication had excluded everyone else with their love.

The hopelessness of trying to find or follow him now had been cemented by his words of that morning: "It's got to be a goodbye, not a good night."

The voice of her mother circled her mind: "You'll pay for this girl, mark my words. You don't sell yourself without a price. God will punish you, be sure of that." Bitter warnings that Joyce had chosen to ignore. Words from someone who had probably never in her life known what love was in any fullness. Judgemental, ignorant and unloving.

But now, true. After everything, her mother had been right. The price of adultery - a word she hated to use - would now be exacted on her. God would have his say as her unbelieving mother had predicted. Joyce would bow to the inevitable of a future where no one would care for her on any significant level. Not even Jimmy, with his personal brand of childish love.

The room was now dark. Soon her mother would be knocking again, though why she came Joyce did not understand. Perhaps to spit out the last drops of criticism. Perhaps because there was little else in her own life than making other people unhappy. It didn't matter any more. She could come, learn of her son-in-law's death, berate and blame her daughter, be as vindictive as she cared to be. It didn't matter. What did anything matter now? There was no emotion left in her to rail against outsiders. The world outside was too complex for her, celebrating its victory, mourning its victims, putting its life back together again, whilst she could do none of these things. She pulled her jacket round her shoulders and rocked in the armchair.

When her mother finally knocked on the door Joyce ignored it. The knock was repeated, more firmly, but still she felt unwilling to move. The silence and stillness returned. Another knock cut the air and the young woman acceded to its demands. Sooner or later her mother had to know; best get it over with. She moved slowly to the door and flicked on the electric light switch. She knew she must look a mess, but what did it matter. For a moment she wondered what first words would pass between her mother and herself and how she would tell her of Jimmy's death. The thought passed and she opened the door slowly.

"I'm sorry my darling, but I just had to see you for one last time".

THE RESCUE

I arrived home soon after dark. It was raining – heavy, cold October rain. It had rained all day.

"You'll have to go and bring them back home," my wife said. The two other mothers put down their cups and murmured their support. My daughter and two other fifteen year old girls had left that morning to do their Outdoor Pursuits Gold Award hike, the culmination of weeks of planning and preparation for this prestigious achievement. Carrying all their kit – tents, sleeping bags, cooking equipment – they had gone by bus to a map reference in the countryside. There they were to open sealed orders and, following them, walk across country to another map reference fifteen miles further on. They were to keep a detailed log of the journey and prepare "a properly cooked, hot evening meal" at their overnight camp. No other girls in the school had reached this stage in the course, and much depended on the success of the venture for future schemes.

"Jennifer will be telephoning at eight o'clock," my wife reminded me. "When she does I'll find out where they're camping."

"But she won't tell you where they are if she knows I'm going to bring them back."

"She won't know you're going to bring them back. I won't tell her."

"But they'll lose face with the school if they're not allowed to finish the test."

Mrs.Griffiths intervened. "It was quite irresponsible of

Mr.Philpot to let them carry on and worry us like this," she said. "The weather was bad enough this morning. And it's got worse during the day. They should have had the sense to turn back. They'll be cold and tired and they'll be sleeping in wet sleeping bags in their damp clothes. They'll catch their deaths." The tea-cups rattled their assent.

I tried again to reason. "Look, Mr.Philpot's an experienced teacher. If there's anything wrong he's bound to sort it out." The silence that followed was several degrees more effective than counter argument. As a final ploy I reasoned, "Why don't you ring Jennifer's mobile, just to make sure ?"

"They've been told not to use mobiles unless it's an emergency," intervened Mrs.Hamilton, contributing for the first time. I didn't even try to argue against the logic.

The telephone in the hall rang shortly after eight o'clock. My wife went to answer it, leaving the sitting room door slightly ajar. We waited like Florentine conspirators, listening to the murmur from the hall. My wife came back to report. "They're camping at Billington," she said. "They're in a field about a quarter of a mile from the phone box."

"There must be a hundred fields a quarter of a mile from the phone box!" I exclaimed. The mothers frowned in concert at my defeatism.

"The farmer who gave them permission lives right by the phone box," my wife said sharply.

I found Billington, in its cobweb of narrow lanes, at 9.30. The right farmhouse was the fifth I knocked at. I would find them easily, the farmer assured me tersely, somewhat irritated at having to open the door at this time of night. They were down the second lane on the left past the church. The gate's top bar was painted white. The door closed firmly.

I found the potholed lane and bumped down it, wondering at all the benefit my car was receiving from the trip. The gate was on the right. The rain was so heavy that I had to lower the driver's window to be sure it was the right one. It was wired to the gate post and having fumbled for a minute trying to unloosen it I resorted to climbing over it. On the other side I dropped into a water-filled tractor rut. My shoes filled with wet mud. I stared wide-eyed into the darkness and pathetically shone my torch, which did nothing other than emphasise how hard the rain was beating down. I couldn't see any tent. The only course was to follow the line of the hedge, which I did, walking through ankle-deep grass. The wind was gale-force.

The tent was in the lee of a bank on the third side. It was calm in the lee, and I heard the girls before I saw their tent, a small light shining from inside.

They were singing.

The singing stopped.

They laughed.

Then they started singing again.

The absurdity of it all struck me like a blow. They, the objects of parental concern, were snug and warm, well-fed and happy enough to sing. I, their rescuer, was soaked through, rain dripping down my spine, cold and miserable enough to weep.

I squelched stealthily away like a defeated animal. As I left the shelter of the bank a gust of wind swirled my hat off my head and out somewhere into the blackness. I let it go and drove home soaked and shivering. I had forgotten to raise the driver's window before I searched the field. The driving seat was a puddle.

I was in bed the next afternoon when Jennifer arrived home. I heard her talking to her mother in the kitchen. I could hear laughing, the high-pitched hysterical laugh of those enjoying the discomfort of a fellow human being.

Jennifer came up to see me. She looked so fit and well. I felt so ill.

"I've caught a cold", I said, sniffing miserably.

"I know," she said grinning, "I've caught your hat."

ISBN 141202972-4